DEVELOPMENT OF AN INTERCESSOR DEVOTIONAL

Leila Dianne Scrivner

ISBN 979-8-89043-195-0 (paperback)
ISBN 979-8-89043-196-7 (digital)

Christian Faith Publishing
832 Park Avenue
Meadville, PA 16335
www.christianfaithpublishing.com

Printed in the United States of America

PROLOGUE

This book inspired by the Holy Spirit is to raise up the intercessors within the body of Christ, who may be ignorant to intercessory prayer like I was three years ago. Intercession is one of the two callings that all believers have been called to. The other is that we are to be ministers of reconciliation. Well, I believe that intercession is somewhat of a prerequisite to ministering reconciliation to those who are lost and not at peace with Father God through Jesus Christ. Intercession is pleading on behalf of another. Why do we need to plead on behalf of others? Scripture says in Revelation 12:10 that we have an accuser who accuses us day and night. If there is something in the spiritual realm accusing us day and night, shouldn't we talk to God the Father, who is also a Righteous Judge, just as earnestly on behalf of ourselves and the brethren?

The first thing the Lord strategically had me learn was the format of prayer. I remember on February 2014, I was mandated by our church to serve within some capacity. At that time, I thought vacation Bible school crafts would be a good fit for me. Little did I know, I had been placed on the leadership committee instead of the volunteer team. I had no idea what I was going to do; church in that capacity was relatively new for me at that time. One of the women serving on the leadership committee with me was what everyone called "a prayer warrior," and our church's first lady asked her to teach us all how to pray before we began discussing vacation Bible school plans. This sister gave a prayer outline acronym ACTS, which stands for Adoration, Confession, Thanksgiving, and Supplication. At that point in my life, I could honestly say that I never knew how to pray. I had been water baptized and had made a profession of faith when I was twelve years old. I had been in and out of church over the course of my life; learning to pray was never a subject that I encountered.

Bible study, sure. Small group fellowships, sure. Serving in a ministry, sure. But again, never had there been an emphasis on learning how to pray and the importance of prayer.

The second thing the Lord strategically had me to learn was that prayer does truly change things, not only in the spiritual realm but in the natural realm as well. He led me in September 2015 to watch the movie *War Room*. This movie sparked a desire in me to see God change things in me and through me. Around the time that I watched this movie, it had been a year since the Lord convicted my husband and I to trust Him with our fertility. We had yet to conceive a year later, so in that sense, I thought that would be a good place to start pleading to the Lord for change. Praying confidently with and for others progressively grew from that first time in my newly established prayer closet. There was a seed planted in me at the 2014 Vacation Bible School Leadership Meeting that was watered by the movie *War Room*. My progressive confidence in prayer was the increase that the Lord promises He would bring in 1 Corinthians 3:6–8. That fall, my increase in prayer transitioned from me not even knowing what to say to God those first few meetings in my prayer closet to written prayers daily in my journals, to offering virtual written prayers to others on social media, to being invited to join the prayer ministry at our church after our pastor asked me to close out a harvester meeting that spring of 2016.

Lastly, the Lord connected me to four other believers in the DFW area through a Christian Facebook group that He told me to begin for ladies all over to inspire one another through His Word. Four of us began to meet up and develop close friendships. We could call on one another for prayer and be there for one another at important events such as water baptism. Fast forward to summer of 2016, one of those sisters, who I had come to learn was an intercessor, was available to pray for me by phone after a demonic manifestation had come over me following my discipleship of another sister in Christ. After this sister prayed for me, she began to teach me some of what she had come to learn as an intercessor. She taught me about inner vows and agreements with demonic power that I might have come into partnership in my life, which could have brought on that manifestation during the discipleship of that other sister in Christ. She also shared teachings with me on prayer that shifted atmospheres in regions and territories. Wow is all I could say! I never knew that there was so much to prayer and that there were different types of prayer, all for the glory of God.

As an intercessor, I began to understand that fasting was also an important key to my prayer life. Jesus told His disciples in Mark 9:29, "This kind cannot come out, except by prayer and fasting." After the Lord began to show me the spiritual condition of myself and others, He began to lead me to various fasts, especially in 2017. I would say that year, I fasted more than I could recount eating. There were various types of fasts that He led me into for specific reasons and seasons. There was an Esther fast that He led me to do to see break through in the area of salvation for one sister in Christ. But there are other fasts, such as the twenty-one-day Daniel fast to reset in the new year and a seven-day-no-food fast that fall to give my husband and me more revelation into the Lord's redemptive plan concerning our adulterous beginning. Also, a forty-day dusk-to-dawn fast—one in the winter, and one in the summer. In the winter fast, the Lord used to give me clarity and increase my faith during the process of Him purchasing us our home against all Earthly logic. In the summer fast, the Lord used me as a catalyst to encourage my sister to go deeper in her faith journey. I must say these past three years had been exciting to watch the Lord grow me in the gift of prayer, intercession, and even the prophetic.

As I drew nearer to the Lord in prayer and intercession, He began to increase speaking to me through dreams, visions, and audible manifestations of His voice. After the disciples were waiting and praying in the upper room on the day of Pentecost, the Lord spoke through Peter in Acts 2:17 that "in the last days, 'I will pour out my Spirit on all people. Your sons and daughters will prophesy, your young men will see visions, your old men will dream dreams. Even on my servants, both men and women, I will pour out my Spirit in those days, and they will prophesy. I will show wonders in the heavens above and signs on the earth below, blood and fire and billows of smoke.'"

I added this section to the prologue as an encouragement to believers that as we pursue God and draw near to Him, He is faithful to draw near to us, answer us, and reveal His plans to us.

After four years of walking surrendered to the Lord and three years of learning and practicing spiritual warfare through prayer, He taught me that obedience to personal revelation of His written word made my warfare prayers even more effective. Obedience to God is an expression of our love for Him (1 John 5:3) and allows His Holy Spirit to operate in more power through us (2 Timothy 3:5). He showed me in Psalm 91:1, "Those who live in the shelter of the Most High will find rest in the shadow of the Almighty."

I learned that the original sin is what drove Adam and Eve from the Garden of Eden. This place was God's shelter, where He dwelled; it was set apart from the outside world for His original two people, and there they did not have painful toil (Genesis 2:8, 3:23). Their disobedience left them outside of God's shelter, open to the outside world, which consisted of pestilence, plague, terror, thousand and tens of thousands being against them, disaster, harm, lions, cobra, and serpents (Psalm 91:1–16). Another direct scriptural correlation between obedience and rest in His shelter is in Hebrews 4:10–11: "For all who have entered God's rest have rest from their labors, just as God did after creating the world. So, let us do our best to enter that rest. But if we disobey God, as the people of Israel did, we will fall."

Specifically, the effectiveness of warfare prayer is referenced both in James 5:16a, as we are encouraged to confess our sins to one another for healing, and 1 John 1:9, as we are encouraged to confess our sins to our faithful and just God for cleansing of all wickedness. Furthermore, James 4:7 again highlights the two-part effectiveness of our prayers with, "Submit yourselves, then to God. Resist the devil, and he will flee from you." In conclusion of this point, James 5:16b says the prayer of a righteous person is both powerful and effective. And lastly, in the words of Jesus in John 15:7–8, "If you remain in me and my words remain in you, ask whatever you wish, and it will be done for you. This is to my Father's glory, that you bear much fruit, showing yourselves to be my disciples."

I believe that discernment is another key factor to proper stewardship of the intercessory gift. Discernment and intercession coupled can shift the spiritual atmosphere over territories and regions or, in other words, "till the soil" for the Holy Spirit to encounter the hearts and minds of the people in those territories and regions. Territories and regions can include your church, workplace, home, & your home. Here is a powerful testimony of the gift of discernment at work, coupled with intercession, to conclude this section.

In April of 2019, at a church my family and I attended one Sunday, the Lord put on my heart that the pastor was teaching from an academic knowledge and not by the revelatory knowledge as given by the Holy Spirit. I took this "Holy Spirit download" to my prayer closet and then disclosed this information to three confidants as my witnesses. To my surprise, as I would say the Lord is still refining my giftings, that same pastor a few months later in June 2019 confessed to the congregation that he never had a prayer closet or "tent of meeting" during his teaching out of Exodus 33. He then said that once the Lord prompted him to create his "tent of meeting," he prayed a personalized version of Moses's prayer from Exodus. He repeated twice during the service that on that day, he cried to the Lord, "I want to know You and Your ways, not just academically. Lord, show me your glory." I knew the Lord was showing me in public that He had answered my prayers in private just as Jesus promised the Father would do for His children in Matthew 6:6.

This book is outlined to inspire each of you for seven days through Scripture, personal testimony, activation of discussed concepts through prayer, and prayer journaling pages for you to get started in intercession. There will be prayer for finances, marriages, fertility, faith, government, and many more topics that will touch the various aspects of your life. Additionally, I invite each developing intercessor to use the blank pages given at the end of each chapter to join me in prayer. Jesus said, "Again I say unto you, that if two of you shall agree on earth as touching any thing that they shall ask, it shall be done for them of my Father which is in heaven" (Matthew 18:19–20). James 5:16 follows up, "The effectual fervent prayer of a righteous man availeth much." May the Lord bless those who become readers, hearers, and doers of God's word through the message of this devotional.

DAY ONE

The Format of Prayer

Adoration

This is praising God for we know Him to be not only through personal experience or encounter, but also based on who His written word illustrates and characterizes Him to be. Psalm 100:4b says that we enter His courts with our praise or adorations of who He is and who we know Him to be. This must be our greeting to the ruler of all heaven and Earth. Think about when we are in an earthly courtroom and the judge enters. We are required to greet him with the words "honorable," and we are expected to rise in his presence out of respect. We are expected to make it known that it is an honor and a privilege to be before him or her. When we have an earthly frame of reference, it makes it a little easier to understand how to approach a holy God, who is honorable, faithful, and just more than any human could ever be, even an earthly judge!

Some scriptural examples of praise or adoration:

Genesis 16:13. Hagar came to know and encounter God in the wilderness fleeing for the life of her and her unborn son. She acknowledged Him and adored Him as El Roi, "you are the God who sees."

Psalm 103:1–5. King David, over the course of a life fleeing from his predecessor, falling from God's grace into the sin of adultery and the painful generational consequences of his actions, came to bless the Lord and His holy name with all of His soul. He came to know God as the One with many benefits, such as the forgiver of his inequities, the healer of his diseases, the redeemer of his life from destruction, the One who crowned him with loving-kindness and tender mercies, who satisfied his mouth with good things, and restored his youth.

Acts 4:24. Peter opened his prayer with adoration like this: "Lord, you are God, who made heaven and earth and the sea, and all that is in them."

Luke 11:2. Jesus taught the disciples to adore our God as our Father in heaven, whose name is to be hallowed.

As you remember your past and present encounters with the Lord, meditate on who He was to you in those encounters. As you read His Word, meditate on the testimonies of who He is based on the understanding of your reading. Then when you engage Him in prayer, enter into His gates with thanksgiving and His courts with praise for who He has revealed Himself to be to you through encounter and scripture.

Confession

Daily, we fall short of the glory of God. The truth is that our flesh is weak, despite the willingness of the spirit to please God. Galatians 5:19 NLT lists the fruits of our sinful nature, which are sexual immorality, impurity, lustful pleasures, idolatry, sorcery, hostility, quarreling, jealousy, outbursts of anger, selfish ambition, dissension, division, envy, drunkenness, wild parties, and other sins that are similar in nature. Then in contrast, Galatians 5:22 NLT lists the fruits of the Spirit. These are love, joy, peace, patience, kindness, goodness, faithfulness, gentleness, and self-control. All these fruits can be summed up as righteousness, peace, and joy, which is the kingdom of God or fulfillment of the law in the Holy Spirit, according to Romans 14:17. These scriptures challenge us to look daily at our lives and match each of our actions to either being flesh or Spirit.

Psalm 51:17 says that God will not despise a broken spirit nor reject a broken and repentant heart. Whether these sins are just thoughts or become actions or both, daily, we should look at the Scripture and be heartbroken for how we have fallen short of the fulfillment of God's law through His Holy Spirit, then confess to

Him. In 1 John 1:9–10, it says, "If we confess our sins to Him, He is faithful and just to forgive us our sins and to cleanse us from all wickedness. If we claim we have not sinned, we are calling God a liar and showing that His word has no place in our hearts." His word hidden in our hearts is the new covenant in Jesus that Hebrews 8:10 says: "But this is the new covenant I will make with the people of Israel on that day, says the Lord: I will put my laws in their minds, and I will write them on their hearts. I will be their God, and they will be my people."

To summarize, confession of sin should be a large part of our daily prayer lives, especially if we desire our prayers as intercessors to be classified as fervent and effective (James 5:16).

Thanksgiving

Not only is it God's will for us to be thankful in every circumstance, according to 1 Thessalonians 5:18, but giving thanks also ushers us into the gates and courts of heaven, according to Psalm 100:4, which is where we need to be in order to be before God's throne of grace to receive mercy and find grace to help us in our time of need. Whether it is grace and mercy that we seek to find for us personally or of others who we may be interceding for. Note that thanksgiving is not only to be expressed in prayer, but also an expression of our daily lives in every circumstance.

Supplication

This is an entreaty or inquiry of the Lord. It is also synonymous with prayer, questions, request, petition, and an appeal. Why is it (important) to ask, petition, pray, or request of God? And even more, why is it to ask of Him with a repentant heart and a humbled spirit? As intercessors, we desire to see God sovereignly change things in the lives of people, circumstances, or regions generally. Well, James 4:2b–3 says that "you do not have because you do not ask God. When you ask, you do not receive, because you ask with wrong motives, that you may spend what you get on pleasures."

Examining these verses as they relate to an intercessor, we need the Lord to reveal the motivations in our hearts for what or who we are interceding for. Are our intercessions to satisfy a carnal desire or manifest the glory of God in the life, region, or circumstance that we are interceding for? What is our driving force for passionate prayers? Is our driving force for the love of God and to see His glory? Is fear our driving force? Is selfish gain or ambition our driving force? Before we make our requests known to the Lord, let us regularly ask, just as David in Psalm 51:10: "Create in me a pure heart, O God, and renew a steadfast spirit within me."

Father, thank You for teaching us, as disciples of Jesus, how to pray to You boldly before your throne of grace and receive the mercy and grace that we need in our times of need. You are holy and pure, steadfast in love, generous in wisdom, abundant in grace, and everlasting in mercy. We come to You in agreement with Your word in Jeremiah 17:9, that our hearts are deceitful above all things and desperately wicked. Create in us a pure heart and renew within each of us a steadfast spirit. We ask that You be watchman over the regions, people, and circumstances that You have assigned each of us to so that we do not watch in vain, according to Psalm 127:1–2. We invite You to lord over us as watchman, teaching us how to pray fervent and effectual prayers that manifest Your glory on the earth and are fueled by our love for You and all that You love. In Jesus's name. Amen.

Discernment

The second order of business in being developed as an intercessor is to discuss and pray for discernment in the Spirit. As mentioned in the introduction, discernment is one of the most important gifts that is intended to be coupled with the gift of intercession. Discernment is a characteristic of the Holy Spirit that is given to lovers of God, according to Proverbs 20:12. Jesus gave two commandments to his disciples in Luke 10:25–28: to love God with all of our heart, soul, strength, and mind then to love our neighbor as ourselves. Proverbs 20:12 alludes to the fact that once we come to love God to this degree, which is really an obsession for a lack of a better analogy, we begin to develop eyes to see with spiritual discernment and ears to hear what the spirit of the Lord has to say. To love God to this degree requires us to love our neighbor as ourselves. 1 John 4:20 suggests that it is difficult to claim that we love God, whom we have never seen, yet hate our brother or sister, whom we have seen, without being a liar.

> Lovers of God have been given eyes to see with
> spiritual discernment and ears to hear from God.
> (Proverbs 20:12 TPT)

The enemies of discernment:

1. Confusion
2. Disobedience
3. Doubt

4. Fear/Anxiety
5. Hastiness
6. Ignorance of God's nature and character (accusation and condemnation are not the voice of the Lord)
7. Lack of spiritual feeding on God's Word
8. Pride

The first steps that I would take in asking, seeking, and knocking for an increase in spiritual discernment would be to ask God in prayer some very vital questions of our faith. Psalm 19:12–14 says:

> But who can discern their own errors?
> Forgive my hidden faults.
> Keep your servant also from willful sins;
> may they not rule over me.
> Then I will be blameless,
> innocent of great transgression.
>
> May these words of my mouth and this meditation of my heart be pleasing in your sight,
> Lord, my Rock and my Redeemer.

#1 *Ask the Holy Spirit to reveal to you if you really do love Him with all your heart, mind, soul, and strength.* If He answers no, ask Him to show you the things, past or present, in your life that have hindered you from loving Him in this capacity. Ask Him to give you more grace which, according to James 4:6, is reserved for the humble to overcome the things revealed and have ruled over us.

#2 *Ask the Holy Spirit to reveal what it practically looks like in your life to love Him to this capacity.* Some help from the Scripture:

> And this is love: that we walk in obedience to his commands. As you have heard from the begin-

ning, his command is that you walk in love. (2 John 1:6)

Some believers reference this next verse when it comes to finances, but I would like to believe that God is more interested in all of me than He is in my pocketbook. If He has all of me, then He has my money too. There is no good thing that I would withhold from Him as there is no good thing that He would withhold from me.

Each one must give as he has decided in his heart,
not reluctantly or under compulsion, for God
loves a cheerful giver. (2 Corinthians 9:7)

Once we give all of us as a living sacrifice, according to Romans 12:1–2, we can then test and approve (or discern) what God's good, pleasing, and perfect will is for our lives.

#3 *Ask the Holy Spirit to increase in you the gift of spiritual discernment to effectively intercede in a way that brings forth the will of God and His kingdom here on Earth as it is in heaven.* If you have gotten to this point and have yet to see the manifestation of discernment, keep asking the Holy Spirit the three questions in this chapter. Do not give up and decide in your heart that the gift is not for you. If you have the desire for the gift, that desire came from the Lord, according to Philippians 2:13 NLT, which says that "God is working in you, giving you the desire and the power to do what pleases him." Does it please God for us to pray down His kingdom and will here on earth? Absolutely! Otherwise, Jesus would not have told the disciples to pray that way in Luke 11:2. In 1 Corinthians 12:7–11, it says that the gift of discernment is from the Holy Spirit, who dwells in each of us and distributes the gift freely as He chooses. I will say again, if it is your desire to intercede with discernment, then this desire is from the Holy Spirit, and you can call on Him for the power to operate in the activation of this gift.

#4 *Lastly, testing the spirits (discernment 101).* Jesus says that His sheep hear His voice, they follow Him and do not follow the voice of a stranger (John 10:4–5, 27). One John 4:1 encourages us to test every spirit to discern if it is from God because many false prophets have come into the world. In one of the darkest hours of my life in trusting God with the fruitfulness of my womb, I heard the Holy Spirit speak for the first time in my life since I first came to believe in Jesus as the Christ and was baptized.

When I was on the verge of walking away from faith in Jesus Christ and church again, I heard the voice of the Holy Spirit telling me, "Be thankful and truly be thankful. Post something you are thankful for every day on social media until your perspective changes on how blessed you are." Later, through VeggieTales' cartoon, I found out that what was spoken to me that day was a scripture. VeggieTales quoted 1 Thessalonians' "a happy heart is a thankful heart" on 1 of their episode advertisements. That scripture, in addition to my change of heart through my thanksgiving posts, confirmed that I had truly heard the voice of God that day. This was the beginning of the Holy Spirit teaching me to discern His voice. Scripture says that evidence of a true prophet is that if the thing spoken comes to pass, it is a word of the Lord, and if not, then it is not of Him (Deuteronomy 18:21–22).

Father, we believe that every good and perfect gift comes to us from you in heaven. Grant us the grace to believe that You are not a respecter of person in Your distribution of Your good and perfect gifts. You give freely to the just and unjust, the good and the wicked, according to Matthew 5:45. As we seek You for the gift of discernment in order to be more effective as intercessors, who call down your kingdom and your will to earth, distribute, activate, and empower us in this gift as it pleases You. Also, as we seek You for this gift, let that not be the primary motivation of our hearts. Let the motivation of our hearts always be to first love You with all that we are and have, as You first loved us with all of You, not holding back anything. Teach us how to practically express to You daily all five of Your love languages: quality time, personal touch, gifts, acts of service, and words of affirmation.

We are created in your image and likeness. If we need our love languages ministered to us daily in order to feel loved, help it resonate with us that You desire the same. Any of the enemies standing against us, receiving and operating in greater measure the gift of discernment, Lord Almighty, King of glory, exalt our head above them. Move in our hearts with power to offer You rejoicing and praise as we receive freely from You what we ask. In Jesus's name. Amen.

DAY THREE

Faith

Now faith is confidence in what we hope for and assurance about
what we do not see. This is what the ancients were commended for.
And without faith it is impossible to please God, because
anyone who comes to him must believe that he exists
and that he rewards those who earnestly seek him.

—Hebrews 11:1–2, 6

If you are reading this book, then it is highly likely that you
have put your faith in Jesus Christ. It is likely that you believe that
He exists, but the second part is where I believe most believers are
shaky in their faith. Most of us, I would say, are uncertain that He is
a rewarder of those who earnestly seek Him. I would say that we may
even doubt that He is the giver of good and perfect gifts, especially
if those good and perfect gifts are not what we expect or don't make
us feel good. Most of our belief in God is not based on the truth of
His word, but on the perception of our own personal experience or
someone else's. As believers who have been chosen as intercessors
or watchman, a living faith with our deeds as evidence is essential.
James 2:14–26 tells us that just belief in God is a demon-level faith
and that as the offspring of Abraham, we need a faith that is credited
us as righteousness. This faith, according to these verses, is only evi-
dent through our deeds that glorify our Father in heaven.

Let me tell you about my Abraham moments, which is the
moment I chose to love and serve God wholeheartedly by faith. In
June 2014, I met a woman who shared her testimony with me about

trusting God with her fertility and making disciples of her now eight children as Jesus commissioned us to do. My husband and I had just began attending a church regularly in February of the same year, so neither of us had a foundation or commitment to Jesus Christ or His church at that time. Neither of us prayed or spent time in the Bible, but somehow, I knew that what she said was truth. It became a conviction for me and, then gradually, for my husband also.

At the time, our daughter had just turned one year old. We were preventing any subsequent pregnancy at that time because I had made up in my mind that I wanted to breastfeed her for at least two years, if possible. My doctor and others warned me that a subsequent pregnancy could interfere with my milk supply for her. So we prevented pregnancy until the day that the Spirit of truth convicted my soul that beautiful day in June. Immediately, when I returned to my car, I told my husband that I was fully convinced that we needed to trust God with our fertility. We immediately stopped preventing pregnancy and halfheartedly trusted God with our fertility for the next year. We said to ourselves that if it would happen, then fine, and if it wouldn't, even better because I still wanted to breastfeed my firstborn into her second year.

As a year went by, I found that I still had not conceived a baby. I became angry at God for a second time in my life, and just before I chose to walk away from the church and putting my trust in Him again, He personally spoke to me in August 2015. From that point forward, I committed myself to seek the Lord wholeheartedly, not just for what I wanted but for Him to come and to truly know the One who spoke to me on that day. My church planted the seed that taught me how to pray, and the movie *War Room* watered the seed in 2015. Then, at a Joyce Meyer conference in October of that same year, I was led to pray by faith to be baptized with the Holy Spirit, which empowered me as a witness of Jesus Christ. First, after being baptized with the Holy Spirit, I was strengthened to share my testimony of healing on social media boldly and without shame. Then, He led me to start a social media group that brought me together in fellowship with about six to eight other ladies. One of those ladies was a seasoned intercessor, who had been through personal deliverance and served in a deliverance ministry.

On January 2016, my first-born daughter became very ill. She became covered with a red rash all over her body and even was unable to walk for a short while. We took her to the hospital, and she was prescribed several medications to address what seemed to be some kind of systemic allergic response. She was only two and a half years old at the time, and she would vomit the medicine when we administered it. I began to get so afraid that she would not recover, and I could feel God's peace trying to leave my spirit. In the middle of my husband trying to make an attempt to give her the medications, I went into another room, bowed my knees, and laid her life on the altar of God. I truly indeed had an Abraham moment. I told the Lord that I desired my daughter to recover, but I was also willing to let her go. His peace and presence was what I desired to remain in my mind and heart more than anything else at that time. This was a huge breakthrough in the idolatry of my heart. I had always made my daughter an idol, and the expectancy of another baby had become an idol at the time as well. In that moment of the testing of my faith, I was willing to lay down everything for the peace and presence of God to remain in my life. My heart, mind, and soul needed to love Him, were desperate to love Him, and remain in that love that I had only recently come to know after a lifetime of not knowing it.

Father, you are the lover of our souls. To love You with all our heart, mind, soul, and strength is not just one of the two commandments Jesus gave us, but a need that we are all empty without. Increase the faith in every person who reads this book. We don't want to have faith only in seeing You fulfill promises but, more importantly, the faith to lay down everything that has taken first place in our hearts. Give each of us the faith to make You first place in our hearts. The faith to know that You exist and are a rewarder of those who diligently seek You. Reward us with the life of Jesus, a life completely submitted to Your will above our own, and reward us with a heart that is pure enough to see You as we search for You.

To love you with all of our heart, mind, soul, and strength is the greatest need that we would ever need satisfied in our lives. Father, this is what we need faith for. We need the faith to believe that in this love for You, we have no lack, and that indeed this love for You is the greatest need that we need satisfied. Thank you for beginning us and making us whole through faith. In Jesus's name. Amen.

DAY FOUR

Fertility

Now that the foundational principles of intercession have been covered, let us move into specific prayer topics. The first topic we will discuss is fertility! My journey of walking surrendered to the lordship of Jesus Christ was in September 2015 at the age of thirty-four. I have a long history beginning at age twelve of knowing Jesus Christ as my Savior and my healer, but never my Lord until my thirty-fourth year. My history with Jesus, in a brief summary, involved Him saving me from the death trap of teenage sexual immorality and promiscuity and Him healing me of Hepatitis C virus, acquired at the age of seventeen. Despite my knowledge of Him through the Word and my life experience, I again walked through sexual immorality and adultery that led to my failed first marriage. The more I sought the Lord, the more I found Him. The more I hunger and thirst for righteousness, the more I become satisfied in a life surrendered to the will, way, and word of the Lord.

My fertility narrative is one that began with mercy, followed by encounter with Jesus, humility and repentance, and, finally, healing.

God's mercy triumphed His judgment in my life. As an adulteress, God's judgment against such a sin is found in Leviticus 20:10, which says both the adulterer and adulteress should surely be put to death. Proverbs 6:20–35 warns that there is nothing that the adulterer can do to compensate or repay for the wife of another man, which he has stolen, and that the adulterer (paraphrased) "cannot play with fire and not expect to get burned."

Instead of the death and ashes that we deserved because of our unrighteousness, God showed us mercy in 2013 when He blessed and anointed my womb with the crown of life and the crown of beauty, my firstborn biological daughter, after six months of desperation to be pregnant. At the time, I had no knowledge that it was God's mercy. I thought this was what every person who was sexually intimate was entitled to, sometimes earlier than expected or later than expected. However, through my journey of growing more in the fear of the Lord, which Proverbs teaches as the beginning of wisdom and knowledge, I learned that the Word teaches that children are a reward, a heritage. As Matthew 5:45 taught me, the Father of heaven and Earth makes the sun rise on the evil and good alike, and rain is sent to the just and the unjust. If He has predestined you to be His legitimate son or daughter, just and good, then what He sovereignly gets you to do with these truths come through His discipline.

To summarize what I am saying, everyone gets His mercy, the good and the evil, the just and the unjust; however, only those predestined as sons and daughters will be disciplined by Father God. Perhaps the pain and suffering of enduring through miscarriage or infertility for a season has made you question the goodness of God or His love. Maybe even caused you to doubt if it is His will for you to bear a biological child. I have good news! It is God's will, and it is written several times throughout New and Old Testament scriptures. Don't question His goodness anymore because He is good and only gives good gifts, even if that gift is the discipline that comes through the endurance of pain and suffering. Don't question your goodness anymore because as you read, He rewards the good and bad alike. Instead, pray and seek Him—not the baby that you long for. Seek Him and find Him, and know that He is a rewarder of those who diligently seek Him (Hebrews 11:6).

If in you seeking Him He leads you to humble yourself, then humble yourself. He opposes the proud but gives more grace to the humble, according to James 4:6. Why would you need more grace? The grace is needed to not lose hope along the journey of waiting and enduring through suffering. Romans 5:3–5 admonishes us to rejoice in our sufferings, knowing that suffering produces endurance, and endurance produces character, and character produces hope, and hope does not put us to shame because God's loves has been poured into our hearts through the Holy Spirit, who has been given to us. To go through such a process on the journey of building our character and establishing in us Jesus Christ, our living hope, trust me, we need more grace.

Finally, if your praying and seeking Him leads you to an area of repentance, such as it did for myself and my husband, then by all means, repent. Repentance means to turn away from anything that would keep you from the inheritance of the kingdom of God. Not just eternal heaven, but also heaven here on earth.

> Or do you not know that the unrighteous will not inherit the kingdom of God? Do not be deceived: neither the sexually immoral, nor idolaters, nor adulterers, nor men who practice homosexuality, nor thieves, nor the greedy, nor drunkards, nor revilers, nor swindlers will inherit the kingdom of God. (1 Corinthians 6:9-10)

If any of these things may be an obstacle that Satan can use to keep you from the supernatural healing that your body needs to bear fruit or receive the reward promised not only to the good but also the evil—in this case, children—then ask the Holy Spirit to lead you to truth in this area. Reveal to you if any of these things are keeping you from your inheritance, the kingdom of God. Jesus showed us the kingdom. It wasn't only eternal salvation for our souls but also power, righteousness, peace, joy, healing, deliverance, and fruitfulness that would come with abiding in Him.

> If my people, who are called by my name, will humble themselves and pray and seek my face and turn from their wicked ways, then I will hear from heaven, and I will forgive their sin and will heal their land. (2 Chronicles 7:14)

Some of Scripture references: James 2:13b, Proverbs 127:3–4, and Hebrews 12:7–11.

Father of heaven, You are rich in glory. It is to Your glory that Your people called by Your name, be fruitful and multiply. Help us to not only believe but to know, without a doubt, that this is Your will according to Your word. No matter what the culture may suggest, help us to hang onto the truth of Your unchanging word. Father of light, shine light into the dark, desolate, and barren areas of our body, soul, and spirit. Let the light of Your word and the water of Your spirit cause your people to be fruitful in every area of life, especially in the reproduction of righteous offspring. Just like Hannah, from a pure heart, give us the grace that we need after a long season of barrenness to wholly devote our children to walk in Your ways, to trust You with all of their hearts, and to love You with their whole being.

Lord of Hosts, bring down all walls of pride and self-righteousness within the hearts of each of us so that we can humble ourselves and repent of any wickedness that has been a hindrance to us in receiving the fullness of our inheritance. As we pray and seek You, please do not hide Your face any longer. Look favorably upon each of us, who desire to reproduce offspring after our own kind, a holy and set apart royal priesthood. In Jesus's name. Amen.

DEVELOPMENT OF AN INTERCESSOR DEVOTIONAL

DAY FIVE

Finances

This is such a tough topic to discuss and even intercede for, especially in a generation where "the prosperity gospel" is a teaching that has deceived many and led their hearts astray from Jesus the Christ, the way and the truth and the life. So I am going to start this day with recommending each of us to start our financial intercessions by asking the Holy Spirit to examine the meditations of our heart and the words of our mouth.

In Psalm 19:9–14, the psalmist references the fear of the Lord as pure and His decrees as firm and righteous. Then he goes on to discuss how the decrees of the Lord warn us of the things not good for us and reveal to us our hidden faults. He prays for God's grace to keep him away from willful sins and to keep willful sins from ruling over him. He concludes the psalm with asking the Lord to examine the purity of his heart and his words. And finally, that the Lord would empower his heart meditations and the words of his mouth to be pleasing to Him in His sight. His final thoughts are an acknowledgment of the Lord as his Lord, his rock, and his redeemer because these are the attributes of God that he knew to trust in for this prayer to be answered.

Before we begin interceding for finances, whether our own, our city, or others, we must take this important first step with the Lord. Why is it my opinion to make this prayer priority before financial intercessions? In Matthew 6:24, Jesus talks about treasures in heaven as more important than treasures here on Earth. He says, "No man can serve two masters. Either you will hate the one and love the other, or you will be devoted to the one and despise the other. You cannot serve both God and money." Who has ever thought or believed that they have made money the master of their heart? Who would willfully do it, especially if they make claim of Jesus Christ as Lord and Savior? My answer to this is none or very few. Therefore, it is important to go before the Lord, who is the Only one who can accurately examine the purity of our hearts. Jeremiah says in Jeremiah 17:9, "The heart is deceitful above all things and beyond cure. Who can understand it?" Then in verse 10, the Lord says, "I the LORD search the heart and examine the mind, to reward each person according to their conduct, according to what their deeds deserve."

With all said above, I do not believe that earthly riches are evil, nor do I believe that intercessions in the area of finances are evil. I do not believe that makes you prosperity gospel indoctrinated. On the contrary, I believe that it is God's will for His people in exile to prosper, according to Jeremiah 29:4–14. All of us who are in Christ, who live on the Earth, are in exile in a sense because Earth is not our promised land. In heaven, seated with Jesus Christ, is our promised land, according to Ephesians 2:6. Which is why Jesus says in Matthew 6:24 to make treasures in heaven our priority. However, while we are on earthly exile, God expresses to us His will for us in Jeremiah 29:4–14 to build houses and settle down, to plant gardens and eat what they produce, to marry and multiply, for our children to marry and multiply, and to seek peace and prosperity for the city that He has sovereignly placed us in. He says in verse 7, "Pray to the LORD for it, because if it prospers, you too will prosper."

When you do prosper financially or even if you do not prosper financially, how will the Holy Spirit reveal to you the Lord of your heart? Great question! Jesus shows us through the parable of the rich young ruler and his encouragement to his disciples in Mark 10:17–31. When Jesus applauds you for your obedience to your adherence to His commandments to love God and your neighbor, then turns around and asks you to sell all your earthly possessions and give to the poor as a deposit into your heavenly treasure, your response will reveal to you the Lord of your heart.

The rich young ruler showed Jesus that even though his outward actions were righteous according to the law, the God who gave those decrees was not the Lord of his heart. His earthly wealth had become the Lord of his heart, and he did not even know it was revealed to him through Jesus's answer to his question. Jesus went on further to tell his disciples not to worry neither about their position in the kingdom of God nor the earthly treasures they would sacrifice for Him and the gospel. He said not only would the earthly treasures be restored one hundred times in the present age, but they would come with persecutions and, eventually, eternal life in the age to come.

I am going to conclude my discussion on finances with a quote from Paul in Philippians 4:12–13" "I know what it is to be in need, and I know what it is to have plenty. I have learned the secret to being content in any and every situation, whether well fed or hungry, whether living in plenty or in want. I can do all this through him who gives me strength."

When we consider our prayer strategies as intercessors, whether for ourselves, others, or our city, let us first pray for the Lord to examine and empower us in the purity of the meditations of our heart and the words of our mouth. Then pray to Him to give us both desire and power to pursue heavenly riches even more than earthly riches. If our clothes or food or drink are in lack while we are pursuing the kingdom of God and His righteousness, remind Him of what Jesus said in Matthew 6:33. He says that all of those things will be given to those who seek His kingdom and righteousness. Also, once we know and choose Jesus as the Lord of our heart, we can remind Him that in Psalm 23:1, the truth spoken through David is that when the Lord is our shepherd, we have no lack. Then finally, give thanks to the Lord for all that you have, whether your present season is financially poor or abundant. Ask Him to empower you to be content in Him and His gospel, regardless of the season you are in. If you are bold enough, ask Him for the one hundred–fold increase of all the earthly possessions that you have sacrificed for Him and His gospel, *but* do not forget to ask Him for the persecutions that are attached to that promise.

Father, thank you, gracious God, for the lordship of Jesus Christ that not only leads us to eternal life, but also riches in that eternal life with You. Thank you for releasing to us, heaven's strategy for our intercessions in the area of finances. We invite You to investigate our heart, Holy Spirit, and reveal to us who we have made our Lord. With Your power, Lord, our Rock, and our Redeemer, help us make the meditations of our heart and the words of our mouths pleasing to our Father in every prayer that we present to Him as a financial intercession. Give us both the zeal and knowledge to seek the kingdom of God and His righteousness. Increase in us a measure of faith to stand on Matthew 6:33 and Psalm 23:1, and trust that we will never have lack in the Lord our Shepherd as we intently set our hearts to pursue His kingdom and His righteousness.

Help us to be thankful and content, no matter the financial season that we are in, came out of, or are headed into. Help us to resist the devil and stand firm in faith when the persecutions that accompany the one hundred–fold riches that are ours when we give up our earthly everything to follow Jesus the Christ. We want to receive all that Jesus has promised; not just the riches of this age, but also the persecutions promised of this age and the eternal life of the age to come for all who give up everything to follow Jesus the Christ. We ask that our every financial intercession will agree with Your word, Your way, and Your will. Come forth the kingdom of God and the will of God through our financial intercessions as we hallow Your name, our glorious and rich Father. In Jesus's name. Amen.

DAY SIX

Marriage

As the Lord is leading me to write up the devotion for this day and this topic, I must be transparent to say that I do not currently have it together in this area. I just completed a devotional called five days to freedom from anger in your marriage. Each day dealt with a valuable nugget pertaining to marriage, specifically my marriage. Day one addressed when your life looks different than you thought it would. Day two addressed when finances cause you to clash. Day three addressed how to rest in Jesus when we are weary and exhausted in our marriage. Day four addressed when communication is broken. Finally, day five encouraged us to obey God's word to love even when we do not feel loved or loving toward our spouse.

> Two are better than one,
> because they have a good return for their labor:
> If either of them falls down,
> one can help the other up.
> But pity anyone who falls
> and has no one to help them up.
> Also, if two lie down together, they will keep warm.
> But how can one keep warm alone?
> Though one may be overpowered, two can defend
>   themselves.
> A cord of three strands is not quickly broken.
>   (Ecclesiastes 4:9-12)

What I have learned over the course of being married for sixteen years of my entire adult life is that I needed to believe God's word as truth in its entirety, surrender to living my life in obedience to God's word, and, above all things, live in a humble and prayerful relationship with God as my Father. I remember early on in my second marriage, the Holy Spirit speak to me about submission or surrender, which I would use interchangeably. He said, "How can you say that you submit to me as your husband whom you have not seen, if you cannot submit to the one whom you have seen?" Isaiah 54:5 references the Lord Almighty the Holy One of Israel, our Redeemer, the God of all the earth, our Maker as our husband. He has declared Himself as my husband, your husband, and all who have put their faith in Him, Jew or Gentile. When He spoke to me about my submission to my earthly husband those years ago and even today, He merged together the truth of who He is in Isaiah 54:5 with what He expects of us as worshippers of Him in Spirit and in truth, as expressed in 1 John 4:20, which says that we are liars if we say we love an invisible God but not the visible people He has placed in our lives.

There is a direct correlation between our submission and the truth of our love according to the Bible. Jesus says it in John 14:23 that if we love Him, then we will obey the Word (His teaching). The Word of God instructs us wives to submit to our own husbands and for our own husbands to love us as Christ loves the church (1 Peter 3:1–7). Our obedience to this instruction for both a husband and wife is individualized and mutually beneficial. A wife's obedience to her individual instruction is not dependent on a husband's obedience to his individual instruction; however, for the benefit of both and for the glory of God, obedience by both husband and wife is necessary in a marriage relationship. This is the wisdom of Ecclesiastes 4:9–12. The unity of a husband and wife to God's word is the good return for their labor. Our labor in Christ is to be united so that the world will know the Father's love, according to John 17:23.

Jesus also teaches that His authority and power was through His submission to the will and ways of His father. In John 6:38– 39, Jesus's submission to the will of His father empowered Him not to lose any of the disciples the Father drew to Him. In the context of marriage and family, let's consider our children as our disciples and see the authority and power that our heavenly Father gives us through submission not to lose them. In John 5:19–21, Jesus's submission to the ways of the Father gave Him the authority to perform great works, even raising the dead to life. In the same way, the Spirit of God becomes the third cord in our marriage ministry when we submit to the power and authority of the Father through our obedience to His word, His way, and His will, just as Jesus did in His ministry here on earth.

The testimony of my marriage being raised from death to life began on March 25, 2018, and continues through until this day as God stepped in and raised it from the death of its adulterous beginnings into a new life in Him. So based on my personal testimony and the truths of God's word, how do we intercede for marriages, our own, or others?

1. Pray for belief in God's word, way, and will as He has expressed through scripture for you as an intercessor and also for the couple in the marriage(s) in which you are interceding. In Mark 9:23–25, the man interceding for his son saw the deliverance and healing of the Lord when he cried out, "Lord, I believe. Help me with my unbelief!"

2. Pray for the nature of humility to overpower the nature of humanity in ourselves and for the married couples because it is the wise who captures the soul, according to Proverbs 11:30. Humility is the wisdom of heaven, and selfish ambition is the wisdom of humanity, according to James 3:16–18.

3. Pray for repentance, personally for the intercessor and for the married couple. Second Chronicles 7:14 says that repentance is one element necessary to manifest God's healing. Jesus says in John 17:14–19 that He sanctified himself with the truth of God's word for His disciples to also be sanctified. Repentance is the fruit of being sanctified in the truth of God's word. It is turning from unbelief to belief in the truth of God's word, even when it does not fit our own

personal agenda or make logical sense. We can see a picture of repentance through Jesus being tested in the wilderness. Although Jesus was sinless and did not have to repent, the Father used this scene to show us what repentance looks like and the temptation that comes against it.

Jesus faced three temptations in the wilderness. First, He was tempted by pride to use His power to disobey God. Next, He was tempted to exchange the truth for a lie. Perhaps it was to become like all the other religious people of the day, the Pharisees, scribes, and teachers of the law, whose father Jesus said was Satan. The devil offered Jesus all the kingdoms of this earthly realm if He would turn His heart from His father and serve him. Lastly, Satan tempted Jesus to abort His assignment early through the lust of suicide. Jesus knew that he had to go all the way to death on the cross to be in God's will, which would have been Jesus pressing forward through to His upward calling, as Paul speaks of in Philippians 3:14.

As an intercessor, ask the Lord how Satan is specifically tempting you away from repentance through the same or similar schemes, whether in your own marriage or ministry. And just like Jesus, watch angels minister to you in those areas as well as watch the effectiveness of your ministry and the fruitfulness of your marriage shift. Also, begin to ask the Lord to show you the shift in glory of the married couple whom you are interceding for through your own repentance, but also as you pray for them to repent.

4. Pray for you as the intercessor to seek God as well as the married couple. Hebrews 11:6 says that seeking God is one of the components of faith. The Scripture says that when we come to God, we must believe that He exists and that He rewards those who earnestly seek Him. The reward in the context of our intercessions would be answered prayers.

Father God, thank you for the gift and the mystery of marriage. Your word in Ephesians 5:31–32 says that marriage is a profound mystery of Christ and the church. Father, increase Your spirit of wisdom and revelation to us and open the eyes of our heart to greater understand such a profound relationship between our marriages and Christ with His church. As wives, increase our belief in Your word to respect and submit to the authority of our own husband. For husbands, increase their belief in Your word to love their wives as Christ loves the church. Enhance our vision to see the return on the labor of humbly submitting to one another in submission to the authority of Your word. Help us to not fear, but instead to trust in Your perfect love. Increase our awareness of Your presence in our marriage relationship as we invite You in, and help us to rely on Your perfect strength in the daily weaknesses. Pour out more grace to us to repent in areas of our hearts that You may expose as darkened or hardened. As we seek You together in our marriages, let us find You and be deeply satisfied in the truth of who You are, our Maker, Redeemer, Lord Almighty, God of all earth, and Holy One of Israel. In Jesus's name. Amen.

DAY SEVEN

Government

For to us a child is born,
to us a son is given,
and the government will be on his shoulders.
And he will be called Wonderful Counselor, Mighty God,
Everlasting Father, Prince of Peace.
Of the greatness of his government and peace
there will be no end.
He will reign on David's throne
and over his kingdom,
establishing and upholding it
with justice and righteousness
from that time on and forever.
The zeal of the LORD Almighty
will accomplish this.

—Isaiah 9:6–7

When the Lord gave me the final day for this devotional, I admit that I had absolutely no idea on how to effectively intercede for government. Then He spoke to me that the key to effective changes in government is through corporate fasting and prayer. James 5:16 says that the fervent and effectual prayers of the righteous avail much. Let us first focus on the effectualness of prayer for government. Jesus told us in Luke 11:2 to ask Father God to establish His kingdom and will here on earth as it is in heaven. This concept helps us to understand and know what to pray for when it comes to effecting change in government. We do not want to pray for any one political party agenda, but rather pray for God's kingdom and will to be done here on earth as it is in heaven. Why do we want to pray this way instead of from a place of our own personal bias?

> What causes fights and quarrels among you? Don't they come from your desires that battle within you? You desire but do not have, so you kill. You covet but you cannot get what you want, so you quarrel and fight. You do not have because you do not ask God. When you ask, you do not receive, because you ask with wrong motives, that you may spend what you get on your pleasures.
> You adulterous people, don't you know that friendship with the world means enmity against God? Therefore, anyone who chooses to be a friend of the world becomes an enemy of God. (James 4:1–4)

Basing our prayers on personal bias brings worldliness into our prayer closets when our objective in intercession for government is to bring God's kingdom and will to the earth.

> Brothers and sisters, I could not address you as people who live by the Spirit but as people who are still worldly—mere infants in Christ. I gave you milk, not solid food, for you were still not ready. You are still worldly. For since there is jealousy and quarreling among you, are you not worldly? Are you not acting like mere humans? (1 Corinthians 3:1–3)

One can infer that these two referenced passages show us that intercessions through the lens of personal political bias can produce the fruit of unanswered prayers and show us that these intercessions are sourced from the flesh rather than Spirit. Paul tells us to pray in the Spirit at all times in Ephesians 6:18. Why should we pray in the Spirit? In Romans 8:27, it says, "And he who searches our hearts knows the mind of the Spirit, because the Spirit intercedes for God's people in accordance with the will of God."

In summary, laying aside worldly views even if they seem religiously motivated is the key to praying in the spirit of God to invite His kingdom and will on Earth to rest on the shoulders of Jesus, Immanuel, as it is in heaven. Let us examine God's heart for people, especially the people of His house. In Jeremiah 7:5–10, God tells His people to deal justly with each other, not to oppress the foreigner, fatherless, or widow. He tells us to refrain from shedding innocent blood, not to follow or burn incense (offer prayer) to foreign gods, not to steal, kill, murder, or perjure. When we intercede for government, we should pray for governing authorities to be put in place who will establish and enforce laws that nurture and protect the freedom of God's house to worship Him in the ways that He desires as detailed here in Jeremiah.

Now, I want to discuss the *fervency or power* part of James 5:16. That power and fervency comes through fasting. One biblically specific example of fasting powerfully bringing change to government is written in Esther 3:1–7, 10. Haman deceived King Xerxes to sign into law death for any who did not kneel to the king or his royal officials in honor. Once Queen Esther heard of this new law, she called for a corporate fast, in which the Lord released to her over the course of three days a strategy to overturn the wicked law that had been signed by the king to bring death to God's set apart people, who would kneel and honor Him alone.

The next two encouragements for fasting come from Jesus. In Mark 9:14–29 is an example of Jesus healing the son of a man who professed to be a believer with unbelief. Jesus's disciples tried to heal his son, but they could not heal the boy. Jesus referenced in Luke 9:40–41 that the people of this man's generation were faithless and perverse after the man told him that Jesus's disciples could not cast out his son's demon. Perhaps we are not seeing the fruitfulness of our prayers in the Father's will being done or His kingdom come in government because we, too, are a part of the faithless and perverse generation that Jesus is referencing through this man's testimony. As intercessors, it is important to look introspectively as we look to the world we are interceding for. Intercessor is a modern name for priests. In the Old Testament, in Leviticus 4 to be exact, it details the responsibility of the priest, who is responsible for taking the sins of the nation before a Holy God. Many sacrifices had to be made, and the altar of the tent of meeting had to be covered with the blood of these sacrifices. As modern-day priests to Jesus, our high priest, the altar of our hearts need to stay covered in the blood of Jesus. As Romans 12:1–2 says, we need to offer ourselves to the lordship of Jesus Christ daily so that He can transform our minds from the pattern of the world to the mind of Christ, which was fully surrendered to God's word, His ways, and His will.

Another example Jesus gives us of fasting is in John 4:27–39. Jesus brought salvation to many in the Samaritan community through His example and teaching His disciples on fasting in these verses. In verses 31–34, Jesus's disciples offered Him food, in which He responded to them by saying that He had food in which they knew nothing about. He went on to say that His food was to do the Father's will and to finish His work. Above natural food, He desired to reap in a harvest of souls in which He did not sow into. Jesus told His disciples in Matthew 9:37 to pray to the Lord of the Harvest, His Father, to send out workers into His harvest field. Now post-resurrection, Jesus has ascended to the right hand of the Father, and it is time that we, His present-day disciples, fast and pray, just as He told John's disciples in Matthew 9:14–15 on what we would do after His departure. As an intercessor, a priest to our high priest, Jesus Christ, who sits in intercession for us at the right hand of the Father, we must seek Jesus daily for discipleship. We must seek to know and understand His ways and will in our daily reading, meditation, study, and application of the Bible. We must also seek to understand the ways and will of the Father through our secret place and prayer time.

This idea of discipleship from Jesus leads me to discuss the *effectiveness* of our prayers as intercessors or priests. I believe the effectiveness of our prayers is directly related to how deeply we abide in the way and the truth and the life, which is the person of Jesus (John

14:27). James 5:13–20 in my Bible is titled "The Prayer of Faith." This passage is telling us to confess our sins one to another to be healed, which is an agreement with 2 Chronicles 7:14. Sin is what separates us from God. It causes us to cover up in front of Him and hide from Him, then ultimately to leave His dwelling place, just as it did with the original sin in Genesis 3. Our confession of sin, according to 1 John 1:8–10, gives God access to purify us through that expression of our faith. Faith is what God used to credit Abraham as righteous in Genesis 15:6. Our confession of sin proves that His word is in us, and that we believe Him and His word to be true according to verse 10. Jesus said we must abide in Him and His word in us to bear fruit, to ask from the Father and receive, and to show ourselves as His disciples, according to John 15:5–8.

Confession of sin is a key point to us abiding in Jesus and His word in us just, as written in 1 John 1:10. Jesus, the true vine, empowers us to bear fruit when we abide in Him. What was an example of fruit mentioned in James 5:13–20? It is mentioned that Elijah was able to effectively pray for drought and rain in his lifetime. He asked, and he received what he asked for. The demonstration of Elijah's prayers did, in effect, turn back the hearts of sinners from idols to the true and living God, who hears and answers the prayers of faith in those who He has credited as righteous.

> Whoever commits sin also commits lawlessness, and sin is lawlessness. And you know that He was manifested to take away our sins, and in Him there is no sin. Whoever abides in Him does not sin. Whoever sins has neither seen Him nor known Him. Little children, let no one deceive you. He who practices righteousness is righteous, just as He is righteous. (1 John 3:4–8)

Now that we have more understanding of the fervency and effectiveness of our prayers, what it means to pray in the Spirit and righteousness, let us pray for our government in agreement together to be overcome by the kingdom of God and His will.

Righteous and Holy Father, hallowed is Your name. We beseech you to bring Your kingdom and Your will to our government here on earth. We ask You from hearts in this moment—hearts that we offer to You to search out and deal with any anxious and offensive thoughts that would hinder the effectiveness of our prayers for our government. Look upon our motives in prayer and align them with the mind of Your spirit. Upon the revelation of hidden sin, give us the grace to urgently confess our sins and receive Your forgiveness as well as a cleansing of our unrighteousness through the provision of revelation word. Increase us not only in the effectiveness of our prayers through an abiding relationship with Jesus, but also the power of our prayers as You pour out to us, as the body of Christ, the grace to fast more regularly and sacrificially.

We pray for governing authorities to be put in place who will establish and enforce laws that nurture and protect the freedom of Your house to worship You in the ways that You desire. And for any governing authorities who may not establish or enforce laws that nurture and protect the freedom of Your house to worship You in the ways that You desire, use these authorities to uproot and tear down everything in us that has or is fueling unfaithfulness and faithlessness toward You. Thank you for remaining faithful despite our past or present seasons of unfaithfulness and faithlessness. Use our governing authorities in Your way to rebuild and plant us to be a church that Jesus can find faith in upon His return. Whether we deem their ways as good or evil, You are sovereign, and we yield to the truth in Isaiah 55:8, that Your ways and thoughts are higher than our own and hold to the truth, in Romans 8:28, that all things work together for the good of those who love You and are called according to Your purpose. Because of this truth, whether we are in trial or tribulations, we find joy and are growing in the understanding that we truly can do all things through Christ who gives us strength. We can live under leadership that leads us in abundance and leadership that leads us in famine because of Christ's strength (Philippians 4:13).

Help us take our eyes off of the people in office and fix our eyes on You, the One who is unseen and behold the weight of Your eternal glory. In 1 Timothy 2:2, it says, "Pray this way for kings and all who are in authority so that we can live peaceful and quiet lives marked by godliness and dignity." Father, may this verse be revealed to us in fresh ways daily. May it become the daily bread we need in our prayer lives for our governing authorities. As Your first fruit born through the word of truth, we offer ourselves to You in an invitation that You would transform us and renew our minds daily in the light that comes through the truth of this word. As first fruits, may we bear the fruit of peaceful and quiet lives marked by godliness and dignity. In Jesus's name. Amen.

EPILOGUE

Rejoice always, pray without ceasing [do not stop
praying], give thanks in every circumstance for
this is God's will for you in Christ Jesus.

—1 Thessalonians 5:16c18

I have learned over the seasons of my journey with the Lord that my prayer life is directly tied to my faith. In seasons where I have been full of faith, I have also been full of intercession. Never once in the seasons where I have been full of faith was I silent before the Lord, hesitant, timid, or resistant to go before His throne of grace. The opposite has proven true in seasons when my faith reserve would run low or empty then my intercession life would also run low or empty. I would find myself weary and thinking thoughts like, "Why don't they just pray for themselves?" or "What is the point of interceding, what will be will be anyway?" These seasons would always occur when I felt like my big faith let me down. I have been discouraged, insecure, and full of doubt, even unbelief. Now, when we are confident in what we hope for, we tend to pray fervently. When we do not feel like our prayers are effective, the passion and frequency of our talks with God seemingly decrease. Likewise, when we get what we ask for in a season when we have called on the Lord for help, our talks with God tend to decrease in this condition also. As if we have said in our hearts, "Thanks for supplying my needs, I will talk to you again when I need something else."

I used to think to pray without ceasing meant to pray all day and about all things. I still believe this; however, I also see that it means when our faith is tested during trials and tribulations, we should pray about all things even more. Paul wrote this verse to Thessalonica in the same chapter that he wrote about the coming day of the Lord—that highly anticipated great and dreadful day. Paul says that Jesus died for us so that whether we are awake or asleep, we would live together with Him. So whether in trial or in peace, Paul is saying that for the believer, all things are a win-win. Whether dead or alive, on a mountaintop or low in the darkest valley, we are victorious. That is what Christ died for.

David said in Psalm 139:7–8 that whether he was in the depths of Sheol, the spirit of God would be with him. Jesus's death guaranteed us what David was confident of, and the epistles just affirmed this through the proclamation of Jesus's death, burial, resurrection, and all its benefits to believers. When everything seems to be going wrong and we cannot see anything to be thankful or joyful about, let us pray and ask the Lord to show us and to remove the scales from our eyes so that we can see what we do not see when it comes to thanksgiving and rejoicing in times of trial and tribulation. I have had to, at times, pray this prayer, and I can testify of an immediate answer to this prayer every time.

For those who have prayed about the same thing for years and never have seen the prayer answered, keep praying, and pray more. Persist like the persistent widow in Luke 18:1–8. In verse 7 of that parable, Jesus asks, "Will not God bring about justice for his chosen ones who cry out to him day and night?" In Luke 11:1–11, Jesus teaches his disciples to ask and keep asking, to seek and keep seeking, and to knock and keep knocking. When we ask and we grow weary in asking, I challenge us to ask the Lord if there is a different way to ask to get what it is that we desire. When we have sought and do not know where else to seek, I challenge us to ask the Lord to reveal the hidden places that we do not know to look. When we have knocked and are tired of knocking because we have not seen the door opening in a long time, I challenge us to ask for the strength to knock harder and louder until the door comes down or opens for us to walk through. We also might want to ask for the right door to knock on and the right time to knock as well. Jesus guarantees us in Luke 11:13 that our Father in heaven is good and gives good gifts so that when we ask, seek, and knock, we will receive the Holy Spirit.

Let me get this straight. When we ask, seek, and knock, we get the good gift of the Holy Spirit? Great, He is a good gift, but was that what or who I have been asking, seeking, and knocking for? Who is the Holy Spirit? Why would He be the gift the Father gives to an asker, seeker, and knocker? In John 14:16–18, He is our other advocate, sent to help us and be with us forever. He is the Spirit of truth, who the world cannot accept because the world cannot see Him or know Him. But as disciples of Jesus, we know Him because He lives in us and is with us. He is the one who is a conduit for Jesus to come to us, us who have been made children of God and no longer orphans.

This passage highlights a few things about the Holy Spirit and why this is God's response to us asking, seeking, and knocking. He's a help and advocate, One who speaks up for us, guides, and counsels us to ask, seek, and knock on the Father's door in truth. He reveals the motivations of our heart to help us get what we ask for, or He might just redirect us from what is that we think we want or need (James 4:3–6). He helps us discern between our needs and our wants. Our needs are met through God's provision for us from His riches in glory, according to Philippians 4:19 and Psalm 23:2. The things we want come with a cost, and His favor is poured out on the work of our hands, which is the concept of wilderness versus the promised land of the living, revealed in the books of Exodus and Joshua.

Holy Spirit is our gift of leadership and access to God, our Father through Jesus Christ. According to Romans 8:14–17, for those who are led by Him, He entitles us to cry out to our God as Abba Father. He does not make us slaves again to death, which is the payment for the misdeeds of the body. Instead, He is the one wo brought about our adoption to sonship. He testifies with our spirit that we are indeed God's children, heirs of God, and co-heirs with Christ, which means that we will share in both the glory and sufferings of Christ. But the suffering precedes the glory and not worth comparing to that glory, which will be revealed in us at God's appointed time. Holy Spirit is the One who walks with us through Psalm 23's valley of the shadow of death as a presence and a comfort. When our flesh is weak, He is the One who is willing when temptation seems irresistible. He is our help, our comfort, our power, and our God to be honored and not grieved.

He is the power who makes us witnesses of the gospel of Jesus Christ to the utter ends of the earth, according to Acts 1:8.

Leila Dianne Scrivner is a New York–born, Texas transplant, who spent her early years pushing limits and crossing boundaries. After years of living the life of a prodigal, she encountered Jesus Christ and decided to follow Him. In 2015, her journey began with trusting the Lord with her fertility. Currently, Leila is the mother of four children. By profession, she holds a Master's of Science in Physical Therapy and is a certified lymphedema specialist. She has been married for twelve years and renewed in covenant for seven years to her husband, Joe Scrivner, a key person with their local NBA team.

Leila has lived by faith and obedience to the voice of the Lord since 2015, in which He has led her on an adventure that includes becoming a second place winner on the *Wheel of Fortune*, becoming a guitar player, a book author, a prophetic intercessor, and a worship leader in her local church. Leila enjoys cooking, fitness, family time, and travel. Leila is a member of E1A (a local foster and adoption ministry), Unity Queens (a local ministry focused on empowering, equipping, and encouraging teen girls), and I Am the Promise Ministries (a ministry that encourages believers not to give up on the promises of God). Leila has a cup full and running over, but she is passionately in love with Jesus Christ. Through this passionate love she has for Christ came the birth of this devotional. After initially learning the outline of prayer, Leila learned to pray with intention from the *War Room* movie. Then through a Facebook group the Lord led her to create in 2016, she was connected to a friend who taught her about warfare and intercession. Once Leila read 1 Thessalonians 5:16–18, she rejoiced, she gave thanks, and she was determined to pray without ceasing.

Presently, Leila is also a part of the House of Prayer Movement, in which she has led in intercession as well as in worship at local houses of prayer. Walking and talking with the One she loves is her life source. Praying in His authority has been a slow development that she desires to invite each reader to join her in, with the hope of, one by one, bringing forth His kingdom to Earth.